Language Readers

Level 3
Book G
Units 37–42

Jane Fell Greene
Judy Fell Woods

Copyright 2000 (Third Edition) by Jane Fell Greene and Judy Fell Woods.
All rights reserved.

05 04 03   7 6 5 4 3

ISBN 1-57035-441-3
ISBN 1-57035-277-1 Set

No portion of this work may be reproduced or transmitted in any
form or by any means, electronic or mechanical, including
photocopying or recording, or by any information storage and retrieval
system, without the express written permission of the publisher.

Text layout and design by Kimberly Harris
Cover design by Becky Malone
Cover Image © 2000 by Digital Vision Ltd.
Illustrated by Peggy Ranson

This product is in compliance with AB2519 California State
Adoption revision requirements.

Printed in the United States of America

Published and Distributed by

SOPRIS
WEST

4093 Specialty Place • Longmont, CO 80504 • (303) 651-2829
www.sopriswest.com

NORTH HIGH SCHOOL
1550 3RD STREET
RIVERSIDE, CA 92507

Contents

Unit 37   The Longest Walk 1

Unit 38   Fernando to the Rescue 17

Unit 39   Rehearsal for Friendship 33

Unit 40   A Narrow Escape 49

Unit 41   Sabotage at the Internationals 65

Unit 42   Accusation 83

Unit 37
THE LONGEST WALK

UNIT 37

Phonology/Orthography Concepts

- The letter **a** represents two additional phonemes:
  - When **a** follows **w**, it sounds like /o/ in **hot**.
  - When **a** is followed by **-ll**, **-lk**, **-lm**, **-ld**, or **-lt**, it sounds like /a/ in **all**.

Vocabulary

bald	pall	talk	*sew*
balk	palm	tall	*shoe*
ball	salt	walk	*shoved*
call	small	wall	*spirit*
calm	squall	wallet	
chalk	stalk	wand	
fall	swab	wander	
gall	swallow	wash	
hall	swamp	wasp	
halt	swan	water	
mall	swat	watt	

THE LONGEST WALK

Story Summary:

Tom Vonert decides to run away from home. He thinks his reasons are good. But his friends help him to see another point of view.

Tom Vonert swallowed back his tears. He swatted his ceramic shoe bank onto the floor. Years before, the small bank had been a gift from his aunt. "This is really funny," Tom thought, "because Aunt Evanna is the only one who's ever understood me."

Tom calmly shoved the coins and bills into his wallet, thinking of the hundred things that were bothering him: Uncle Wally; his brother, Bo; his parents; his schoolwork; his friends. "How did I ever let myself get into this mess?" he asked himself. "I guess running away *is* the only way out."

Tom had big problems with his uncle. "Baldy-Waldy," Tom secretly called him. Why Aunt Evanna had married such a jerk, he would never understand. His aunt and uncle had lived with the Vonert family since Tom was six. Uncle Wally just couldn't hold a job, and they had no place else to go.

Every day when Tom and Bo got home from school, Uncle Wally would be the only one at home. Wally sat and watched television all day. When the boys got home from school, he had the gall to make them do all his daily chores. He was loud and obnoxious. He never really hurt the boys, but he threatened them, yelled at them, and teased them. Then, he treated the boys like princes when Aunt Evanna or their parents were around.

Bo and Tom didn't dare tell their parents. Uncle Wally let them know that if they breathed a word, their lives would be even more miserable. They had never grasped exactly what he meant, but they had never pushed the issue either.

But Tom's biggest problem at *this* moment was not his uncle, but his brother, Bo. Bo was 18 now, and he was becoming more and more like Uncle Wally. Bo had barely graduated from high school. He never cared about his grades in school. Bo always balked at schoolwork. "Why do homework?" he always challenged Tom. "Nobody looks at it or cares about it. You can get by without doing a lick."

Last year during a soccer game, Bo had thrown a rock at the star player, Dan Burger.

He had almost caused Dan to lose an athletic scholarship to Rutgers University. Now Bo had no friends and no job. He hung around the house with Uncle Wally, watching TV all day. And now when Tom came home from school, he had two people yelling at him instead of one!

"What a loser Bo is turning out to be," Tom realized as he gazed into the bathroom mirror. "One thing's for sure," Tom thought, "*I'm* not going to be a loser." He washed his face in cold water. His tears welled up once more as he shoved his small address card into his shoe. Aunt Evanna had taught him to do that. Her advice to him was always good.

From the top drawer of his chest, Tom grabbed some clothes and stuffed them into his backpack. He spotted a small picture of his family that had been taken when he was only six. That was just before Uncle Wally and Aunt Evanna had moved in. Things had been different back then. Tom had had his own room. Their family had sometimes done things together. They had always cared for him when he was sick. He and his brother had been buddies then. "Those were the good old days," Tom mused. He held the picture for a minute, and then stuffed it into his backpack with his toothbrush.

Tom stalked around the corner of the upstairs hallway. He halted when he heard Uncle Wally and Bo laughing loudly at the TV in the living room. "I'll just sneak out the kitchen door," Tom decided. Silently, he thought, "I'll wander over to the mall before I leave town. Sam said the Rat Pack was playing there this afternoon."

Tom walked down the street. He felt sweat forming on the palms of his hands. He remembered all the many times his palms had felt sweaty before. Every time he had to speak in front of his class, and whenever he was called on at school, sweat would start forming on the palms of his hands. "It's funny, the things you remember when you're running away," Tom thought. Beyond the huge glass doors, at the center of the mall, Tom looked down and spotted some of his classmates. They were wandering beneath the tall rotunda in the center of the mall, down on the lower level. "They'd never understand the way I feel," Tom thought.

Nick, Mat, and Sam, Tom's friends, had been waiting for what seemed like hours. "Didn't the poster say 1:30 PM?" complained Nick. They searched for signs of the "Rat Pack roadies," who had to arrive ahead of the concert stars to set up lights, sound, and equipment for the rock band.

"If you ask me, those posters should have said 1:30 AM," Sam contended, throwing up his hands. Mat noticed Molly Manchester and Tam Turner heading up the escalator toward the main floor of the mall. He called to the girls, "Hey, Molly and Tam, come and sit with us for the concert! We've got plenty of room here next to us."

"Sure, Mat!" they responded in unison. "Save us some seats while we finish our shopping!"

Tom swallowed his tears when he heard Mat call out. He wanted to be with the gang, too. But even though he and his classmates were just an escalator's ride apart, they seemed to be a thousand miles away.

"I think I'll go get a little something to eat," Mat declared with a grin. "A couple of burgers and some fries." Mat was always eating. His parents said his stomach was a bottomless pit.

"Get me something, too," requested Sam, taking some money from his wallet.

"Lend me a buck?" implored Nick. Even though he earned a little money playing his sax with a jazz band, Nick was always broke.

"Sure. I'll bring you something, too," Mat shouted back at Nick as he raced up the purple carpeting of the rotunda steps. "You owe me, pal."

"OK, OK," Nick mumbled. Just then, he noticed Tom. "Hey, Sam, there's Tom Vonert! His face is chalk white! He looks like he just saw a ghost." Nick and Sam shouted up at Tom, but Tom didn't seem to hear them.

The boys' calls went nowhere. The Rat Pack's road gang had just marched into the mall, dragging in unbelievably tall speakers and 100,000-watt spotlights. They immediately began to set up instrument cases, stage backdrops, and bulky equipment.

"Wow!" Sam exclaimed with a wide-eyed stare. "Real roadies! Nick, we'd better hurry and get Tom down here before this thing starts."

"Maybe he doesn't want us to see him. Tom's life isn't great," Nick responded. "That uncle who lives with them is a nut. Have you heard about him?"

Tom was looking around, trying to find a spot where he could see the concert without being seen by the crowd. He just couldn't face his friends.

Sam commented, "From what Tom has said to me, his brother is a real jerk, too. Remember when Bo acted like such a fool at the soccer game?"

"How could I forget?" replied Nick. "I was sitting right next to Mat when Bo threw that rock at Dan Burger. Bo was trying to hit Mat and me!"

"I'm going to try to get him to come down here with us," Sam declared. "Let's see if we can cheer him up. Save these seats while I run up there. I saw him over by the arcade."

"OK," Nick replied, "but hurry up. This place is going to be a zoo real soon. I don't want to get trampled by people looking for good seats."

"You can handle it, Nick," called Sam, racing up the stairs toward the arcade in search of Tom.

"Tom! Tom Vonert!" Sam shouted, as he rounded the corner into the arcade area.

"Oh! Sam," gulped Tom, fighting back tears. There was nowhere to hide. "Hey. What's up?"

"Is everything OK, pal?" Sam asked. "Nick and Mat and I are just waiting for the concert to start. Why don't you hang out with us for a while? Mat's springing for the burgers."

Tom began to feel better. He still had friends he could talk to. But did they really want to listen? Right now he just wished some magic wand could make his problems disappear.

Tom and Sam nearly tripped over Mat, who came stumbling out of the food court carrying a week's worth of food for a family of nine!

"Yo, Sam! Tom! Give me a hand," Mat implored, downing a salty French fry he had just retrieved from the bag.

"Sure!" They each grabbed a bag from Mat's overloaded arms. Heading back toward their seats, they all talked about the Rat Pack's latest CD.

"Sure does take a long time to get ready for a gig," observed Sam, salting his own French fries and pouring extra ketchup on his cheeseburger deluxe.

"Thanks for the grub," Tom said. "You guys just can't imagine what's been happening."

"You said something before about your uncle and Bo getting tight," Sam said. "What's up now?" Sam always managed to calm his friends down when they got into some sticky situation.

Tom spat it out. "I've decided to run away."

"Say what?" Mat choked on a fry.

"That's why I've got my backpack and all. Bo and Uncle Wally keep hassling me. It's just too much. All they ever do is sit around the house and watch TV. When I get home, I have to clean up after them and cook dinner. They said they would get me good if I ever talked to Mom or Dad about it. Uncle Wally is mean and Bo's getting just like him. You all saw what he did at the soccer game."

"But Tom," Mat declared, "don't you think running away from home is a little drastic?"

"Yeah, Tom," Nick interjected. "I ran away once. I think I got as far as Ted's Shell Shop down at the dock. I understand the feeling, though. And it wasn't until I started thinking about what was *really* bothering me that I had a chance to fix it."

"Believe me, I understand what's bothering me," Tom cried. "Uncle Wally and Bo are driving me crazy!"

"Then you need to talk to somebody else. What about your Aunt Evanna?" Sam suggested.

"Did Bo and 'Baldy-Waldy' say anything about not telling *her*?" questioned Mat.

"Yeah," asserted Sam, wiping some ketchup off his cheek. "It can't get any better until you tell someone. And running away never really helped anyone. Man! I mean, where will you stay? What will you eat? How will you get to school? You shouldn't leave your own house because of them!"

Tom sighed. "You're right. Running away won't solve anything. I've been dumped on enough! I guess I could talk to my Aunt Evanna. I could even get up the nerve to tell my parents . . . ."

A blast of loud music interrupted Tom. It came from the tall black speakers on the left wall.

Molly and Tam squeezed in between Mat and Tom. The friends were soon spellbound by the music of their favorite group. For the first time in weeks, Tom Vonert smiled and enjoyed himself.

When they were leaving, Tom pulled Sam aside. "I owe you, Sam," he said. "I'm heading back home now. This may be the longest walk of my life, but Aunt Evanna will be there now, and I'm going to tell her everything. Tonight, I'm telling my parents. I just can't live this way any more. It's *my* home, too, and I shouldn't be afraid to go there. Ever."

Grasping Tom's arm, Sam added, "Come on. We'll walk with you. Maybe then it won't seem quite so long!" As they wandered together into the late afternoon sun, a weight lifted from Tom's shoulders. All his problems hadn't ended, but now he had the spirit to face them. Thanks to his friends.

Vocabulary Expansion

Describe and define these words and phrases:

hang around	sarcastic	repugnant
hush-hush	treat like dirt	breathed a word
push the issue	offer an opinion	practical advice
ill-bred	compromise	good company
spring for	desolate	get up the nerve

Language Expansion Activities

1. List the reasons Tom had for running away. Make another list of the reasons his friends gave him for not running away. Discuss the list with your group and decide whether or not Tom made the right decision.

2. Create a perfect mall. Write a list of the stores which you would include and tell why. Design the mall using paper cutouts, pasted onto a large sheet of construction paper. Compare your design to someone else's in your group. Be sure to include entrances, exits, and parking lots.

Language Expansion Questions

1. Why did Tom decide to run away? In the beginning, did you think it was a good idea?

2. What items did he decide to take with him? Why?

3. What happened to Tom to make him change his mind? If you were Tom's friend, how could you have helped him?

4. Make a list of the events in the story. How might the events in the story have been different if you were writing it from Bo and Uncle Wally's point of view?

5. Suppose Tom had decided to go ahead with his original plan. Create a new ending for the story.

6. Tom was angry. He felt as if no one would listen to him. Think of some things that you've done when you felt that everyone was too busy to listen to you. Think of ways people can help themselves when nobody else is around for them. Why is having someone to talk to so important?

7. What would you have done if you were Tom? Why?

8. Imagine that you are a guidance counselor for teenagers. What advice would you have given Tom?

9. Tom's friends made him think carefully about running away. Friends can sometimes help us, but sometimes their ideas aren't best. Discuss a time when your friends gave you good advice or bad advice. Explain what you did.

10. What do you think Tom learned from this incident?

Unit 38
FERNANDO TO THE RESCUE

UNIT 38

Phonology/Orthography Concepts
- Phonology/orthography for sound patterns /wor/, /wur/, /kwɑ/
- Phonograms are letter groups that usually represent the same sounds (phonemes).
  - The phonogram **war** represents the sound pattern /wor/.
  - The phonogram **wor** represents the sound pattern /wur/.
  - The phonogram **qua** represents the sound pattern /kwɑ/.

Vocabulary

award	squander	word	both
qualify	squash	work	bought
quality	swarm	worker	buy
quantity	toward	world	straight
quarrel	warden	worm	worn
quart	warm	worry	
reward	warn	worship	
squabble	warning	worst	
squad	warp	worth	
squadron	wart	worthy	

FERNANDO TO THE RESCUE

Story Summary:

Nick's family takes a trip to the Grand Canyon, and Nick's friend, Fernando, is invited to go with them. During their trip down into the world's largest canyon, Fernando becomes a hero—and he learns an important lesson.

The window of the van felt warm. Looking out at the giant cactus spread across the desert, Nando felt both pride and shame. They were returning from the first vacation Fernando Rozas had ever taken. Nick Hopkins had invited Nando to go with the Hopkins family to the Grand Canyon.

Weeks before, Mr. Hopkins had called to ask Mrs. Rozas' permission to take Nando on the trip. Nando had been embarrassed when his mom talked on the phone because her English wasn't very good.

Now he felt ashamed. He understood why his mother had insisted that he learn to speak Spanish well. He admired his mother because she could speak two languages. And he was also proud to recall that his own Spanish had saved a life during their four-day trip to the Grand Canyon.

On the second day of their trip, Mr. Hopkins had arranged to take Nick, Bud, and Nando into the Canyon on donkeys. A park warden had given the group several words of warning before they left the South Rim and began their downward journey. Although the path wasn't straight, it was well worn.

They would have no problem finding their way into the Canyon and back out again.

Nando could hardly remember his own father, but practically worshipped Nick's dad. It was worth the world to Nando to be able to go on this trip. He remembered his mother's words of warning: "Be careful; be polite; work hard to be worthy of the trip; and don't squander your money." He took the donkey's reins and followed Mr. Hopkins toward the path.

"Nando?" Bud was asking. "Nando?" Bud's words were lost on Nando.

Bud was Nick's little brother. Bud was a little shy around new people. He would be in the third grade when school began. He reminded Nando of his younger sister, Maria. She was shy with new people, too. The Rozas family had moved to Jasper just last spring. Nando had made lots of friends, but he worried about Maria. Mostly, she stayed home and did schoolwork.

"Nando? Do you think you could help me get these packs fastened? They're both on straight, but I can't get them buckled."

"Sure, Bud! Then we'd better get going. Your dad and Nick are ahead of us with the park warden, and there are some others waiting behind us."

The two followed the path down into the world's largest canyon. Minutes later, they had entered what seemed like another world. There were no buildings in sight, and the only sounds they could hear were those of insects swarming in the shrubs. "It sounds like a squadron of worker bees!" Nando commented.

"It's a good thing my mom bought us the bug repellent!" Bud responded. Both boys trudged happily along the path, leading their donkeys by the reins. They were headed for a shelter where they would spend the night with their group. Nando pointed out a warning posted along the path: **"DANGER. BEWARE OF FALLING ROCK."**

Three hours later, they reached a rest area. The park ranger told them they were a little more than halfway to the shelter where they would spend the night. It was a beautiful warm summer afternoon, but they began to feel a chill as the sun dipped into the sky over the Grand Canyon's West Rim. Two brothers from Idaho got into a squabble about who was supposed to have packed the jackets.

As the group resumed their trek further into the Canyon and toward the Colorado River, Bud and Nando fell further and further behind. Eventually, they realized that the others in their group were out of sight. "Don't worry, Bud," assured Nando. "The park ranger said that if you got separated from your group, you should just follow the path. We can't get lost."

The two boys talked about Nick, and how everybody admired him. Bud's older brother had been elected president of his class.

Last year, when Nick was in seventh grade, he had had to take a state qualifying test. His teacher had realized that Nick couldn't read—at least not well enough to pass the test. She had sent Nick to a specialist who helped kids who had a hard time learning to read, write, and spell. "Dad said it was amazing," Bud now recalled. "Then, they tested me and said I had the same problem. This summer, Mr. Ranson worked with us. Now we can read and spell better."

When Mr. Ranson had explained about smart people who just didn't learn the same way others did, both brothers had felt relieved. "My dad understood," explained Bud. "He told us that when he was a kid, school had been hard for him, too."

"Listen!" interrupted Nando. "Did you hear something?"

They stopped their donkeys, and for a moment they were absolutely silent. Just as they were about to start back down the path, they heard a faint cry that sounded very far away. "I hear something, that's for sure," agreed Bud. "But I don't know what it is."

"It's a person. And it sounds like someone's in trouble," Nando contended. "We have to try to help."

"But we can't go off the path! The ranger said that if you didn't stay on the path, you could get lost. This place is so big that if you don't stay on the marked paths, you could be lost *forever*! He said if you got off the path, a whole squad of park rangers might not find you." Bud pleaded with Nando to stay with him. This was the worst situation Bud had ever been in, and he was scared.

"We have to keep a level head, Bud. I have an idea. You stay on the path. You'll catch up with the group soon. I'm going to see if I can't find the person who was calling for help. I'll try to keep the path in sight. As soon as you reach

the others, you can tell the ranger, and he can radio back to the South Rim for extra help." Bud begged Nando to stay with him, but Nando was insistent. "Don't squabble about this. We have to help," Nando told him. "That's the one thing I remember about my dad. He always said that people were supposed to help each other. That's part of being a human being."

Nando cut back up through the brush toward the direction the voice had come from. Bud, leading both donkeys, scurried down the path to catch up with the rest of their group.

He tried to keep the path in sight, but soon

Nando realized that he was lost. Ahead, he could hear a man's voice calling, "¡Aquí! ¡Estoy aquí!" Nando

25

realized that the voice was calling in Spanish.

On the rocky cliff above him, Nando spotted the man. The ledge was narrow, and the man was squatting toward the back of the cliff. "¡Señor! ¡Estoy aquí, señor!" called the man.

"¿Se encuentra bien? ¡Ya vengo!" Nando reassured him that he was climbing up to help.

He took a rock pick and some rope from his pack. The group had taken a well-worn path into the Grand Canyon, with a park ranger for a guide, and they had all been assured that no climbing would be necessary. But right now, Nando was glad he had decided to pack his climbing gear just in case.

Nando kept calling to the man in Spanish, reassuring him that help was on the way. Several times, he shouted back toward the direction of the path in English, in hope that someone would hear. "We're over here!" he shouted. "We need help!"

As he approached the high cliff ledge, Nando realized that the man's arm had been squashed by a boulder. At least Nando could talk to him now. The man didn't speak much English, but Nando's

Spanish was fluent. "¿Cómo se llama, señor?" he asked him. The man's name was Juan Velasquez. His wife was in the Grand Hotel up on the North Rim, waiting for him. She would be terribly worried. Could Nando get a message to her?

Nando couldn't admit to Sr. Velasquez that he didn't have contact with anyone. He also couldn't see how he could possibly get Sr. Velasquez down from the ledge with his arm so badly mangled. The man would need both his arms to slide down a rope.

Nando began to feel helpless. But behind him, he thought he heard voices. Or was it an engine? As the noises grew louder, they grew clearer. A helicopter was hovering above them! Mr. Hopkins and a squad of rangers were approaching on foot! In minutes, a rope ladder dropped from the helicopter, and a medic was securing Sr. Velasquez to a stretcher to lift him up into the helicopter.

"¡Gracias, mi joven amigo! ¡Muchas gracias!" Señor Velasquez called to Nando. He asked Nando to promise to return to the Grand Hotel the next day, so that he could thank Nando properly.

Nando promised to visit him. "¡Yo vendré a visitarlo, Señor Velasquez!" he said, waving.

"Young man, you're a hero!" called the head ranger, who was leading the group back toward the path. "Señor Velasquez is a wealthy cattle rancher from Mexico City. He has been missing in the Canyon for several hours, and a large reward has been posted for his safe return!"

"Yea, Nando!" Nick and Bud shouted in unison, patting their friend on the back. Nando didn't feel like a hero, but his friends' admiration felt good.

"Nando is probably gonna be on TV, huh Dad?" Bud asked. "Nando, when you're on TV, will you tell them about how I went down the path to get the others? Do you think they'll want me to be on TV too?"

"Sure, Bud. You're the real hero. You went alone to find the others. Without you, I could never have helped Señor Velasquez!"

Nick ruffled his little brother's blond head. "Yeah, Bud. Mr. V. probably wants to give you about a million pesos. You might be able to retire from school and get a pad of your own."

Mr. Hopkins gave Nick one of his looks. Nick could go just so far in teasing his younger brother before his dad stepped in with fair warning.

The group spent an unforgettable night in a shelter overlooking the churning Colorado River. Memories of the starry night in the Canyon and songs around the campfire would last a lifetime. But Nando and Nick's family would have other memories, too.

Late the next afternoon, when they arrived at the Grand Hotel, Señora Velasquez was waiting for them in the drawing room of the Grand Hotel's Presidential Suite. "My husband is grateful," the lady said in perfect English. "Most especially, he is grateful to the boy who spoke Spanish. He reassured my husband when he had given up all hope of being found. I believe the young man's name was Fernando?"

"Yes, ma'am. My name is Fernando Rozas. But everybody calls me Nando."

"My husband has requested to speak to you alone," said the lady, just as Señor Velasquez was wheeled into the room. The Hopkins family left the room quietly with Señora Velasquez, so that he and Nando could speak privately.

As Señor Velasquez began speaking to him in Spanish, Nando began to sob.

"¿Te pasa algo?" asked Señor Velasquez. "What is wrong?"

In Spanish, Nando explained. "I am ashamed. I have been embarrassed to speak Spanish. I wanted to be like everyone else. I didn't want my classmates to meet my mother, because her English is not very good.

"You have helped me to understand that my mother was right," Nando continued. "Being able to speak two languages is something I can be proud of. I will never again be ashamed of my Hispanic heritage."

No matter how many pesos were contained in the reward envelope that Sr. Velasquez had given him, Nando had received a more valuable reward. He was anxious to get back into the Hopkins' van for the ride home to Jasper and to his mother, Mrs. Rozas—his own hero.

Vocabulary Expansion

Describe and define these words and phrases:

succulent	South Rim	keep a level head
crater	cavernous	words of warning
protagonist	antagonist	one of his looks
apprehensive	crag	communication
Presidential Suite	heckle	go just so far

Language Expansion Activities

1. Go to the library and find several books about the Grand Canyon. Read them with your group and have each student write a descriptive paragraph about the Canyon. Illustrate your writings and share them with each other.

2. Create a canyon using clay or papier-mâché. Try to build paths and shelters. Write a play about a group of people heading down the South Rim of the Canyon. Perform your play for your group.

Language Expansion Questions

1. Find the Grand Canyon in an atlas. What state is it in? How big is it? Why do you suppose it's called the Grand Canyon?

2. Why did Nando have to have permission from his mother to go to the Grand Canyon with the Hopkins family? Did you ever have to get permission from your parents to take a trip with someone else? Discuss your trip.

3. Describe Sr. Velasquez. What kind of a person do you think he was? Why do you think he was vacationing in the Grand Canyon?

4. Explain why Nando felt shame about speaking another language. Can you speak two languages? Why is it *good* to know another language? If you could learn any language you wanted, which language would you choose? Why?

5. Nando's mother gave him some words of warning. Reread what she said to him. Has your mother ever warned you about problems you might encounter? Make a list of the things she has told you.

6. Compare Nando's trip down into the world's largest canyon to Nick's trip. Which boy would you rather have been? Explain.

7. Why do you think people say that going down into the Grand Canyon is like entering another world? How is it different?

8. Suppose Nando hadn't gone to help Sr. Velasquez. How would the story have changed? How would Nando have felt?

9. Nando was a hero. He received an envelope of pesos and hearty congratulations from everyone. But he said that he didn't really feel like a hero. Explain what you think it feels like to be a hero. Why did the story's second sentence say, ". . . *Nando felt both pride and shame.*"? Think of a time when you have felt mixed emotions.

10. Nando convinced Bud that he should go and help Sr. Velasquez. What did he say to Bud? Have you ever had to convince someone to do something they didn't really want to do? Was it difficult to find just the right words? Describe the situation.

Unit 39

REHEARSAL FOR FRIENDSHIP

UNIT 39

Phonology/Orthography Concepts

- Phonology/orthography for sound pattern **ear**:
  - Phonograms are letter groups that usually represent the same sounds (phonemes).
  - However, the phonogram **ear** may represent four different **sound patterns**: /ear/, /er/, /air/, /ar/.

Vocabulary

bear	fear	pear	*people*
clear	gear	pearl	*piano*
dear	hear	rehearsal	*minute*
dreary	heard	rehearse	*mirror*
ear	heart	search	
early	heartily	tear	
earnest	heartless	wear	
earth	learn	yearn	

REHEARSAL FOR FRIENDSHIP

Story Summary:

Lake School's representatives are selected to participate in the state oratory contest. On the day of the contest, a crisis helps them learn the real meaning of friendship.

They could hear the lunch bell ring. Mr. Rosenburg had still not announced the winners. Three winners were being chosen to go to the state oratory contest next month, and Trish Marks and Sis  Turner both wanted to win more than anything on Earth.

It was a dreary day. Searching for their lunch gear, they quietly chatted about the contest.

"My sister, Pat, went when she was in third grade," Trish announced. Pat Marks, Trish's older sister, was always winning something. She was a leader, and Trish had always felt that following in Pat's footsteps was the hardest thing she had to do.

"Isn't third grade the first time anyone can be chosen for the contest?" asked their friend Dick.

"Yeah, I think so," Sis said. "That's why I don't have my hopes up too high."

"Well get 'em up there, girl," Trish reassured. "My dad said that your rendition of Auntie Mame was a stitch! He loved that book."

"Dick," Trish smiled saucily, "Come on. Be Julius Caesar again."

Grabbing his backpack from the floor of the classroom closet and heading down the hallway toward the cafeteria, Dick began, "A friend should bear his friend's infirmities . . . ."

Before he could finish, some fifth grade boys started teasing Dick and grabbed his backpack. Pearl Smith, the assistant principal, stopped the boys. They returned Dick's things and apologized.

"Remember those nights at Trish's house when we all rehearsed our speeches?" Sis asked earnestly, selecting a peanut butter and jelly sandwich from under the glass dome. She put the sandwich on her tray and tried to decide between milk and apple juice.

"I remember how hard it was when you kept searching for just the right reading!" Dick loved

teasing Sis. "You kept wanting to learn Juliet's balcony speech, and Mr. Rosenburg said you should wait until eighth grade to do that!"

"It's better than that dreary old poem you were rehearsing at first!" Sis retorted.

"Well, we can thank Dad's set of *Great Books* for helping us find our readings," Trish said. "But I'm living in fear that he'll find out about the page you tore out of that old poetry book. He really would kill me if he noticed a page missing!"

"He probably won't, though," Sis maintained. "I mean, how often do you think your dad reads all those millions of books on his shelves?"

"You'd be surprised," said Trish, loading her chicken taco with salsa and selecting a pear from the tray. "My dad always has a book in his hands."

"Well," Dick chimed in, "It's a good thing he does. None of us would have a chance if it hadn't been for Mr. Marks and his library!"

Trish had slipped out of the lunch line to search for an empty table. On their way to find her, Sis and Dick chitchatted about their classmate's performance.

"I think Trish was even better today than she was at our last rehearsal," Dick declared. "She has a good chance to win." It had been clear that Mr. Rosenburg saw Trish as a possible winner.

"I just hope she doesn't choke if she gets a chance at the state contest," Sis remarked to Dick. "Trish gets too nervous when she's all worked up. She doesn't realize it, but she's always trying *too hard* to be like her sister Pat."

Sis didn't realize that Trish had just walked up behind her.

"Just what did you mean by that remark?" demanded Trish.

"Nothing. I mean, face it, Trish," Sis implored, "your speech today *was* the best ever!"

"You're not going to weasel out of that remark so easily," Trish said, tears welling up. "You just plain don't think it's good enough to win the speech contest. OK. So you and Dick are better than me. So what?" Trish tore out of the cafeteria, with Sis on her heels.

"Come on, Trish," Sis pleaded. "You can't believe that I was badmouthing you. You're my dear friend, Trish! Please don't be mad!"

It was no good. Trish's feelings were always easily hurt, and she couldn't bear it when she heard her best friend comparing her to her older sister.

By the time lunch had ended and the students were headed back to their classroom, the finalists' names had been posted. Everyone raced to the door to see who would get to go to the state contest.

The next week was a flurry of practice and more practice for the six Lake School finalists. Each afternoon after school, they had to report to Mr. Rosenburg's room, where he and Miss Pitt worked with them, helping them to memorize and refine their deliveries.

Three of their six finalists were just third graders. Lake School would be well represented at the state oratory contest for years to come.

Practice was fun, but there was heartache, too.

Sis kept trying to talk to Trish, but Trish wouldn't speak to her. When Trish had overheard Sis's conversation with Dick, she had thought they were criticizing her heartlessly. But they really hadn't meant to criticize.

While Dick was reciting, "A friend should bear his friend's infirmities . . ." for the thousandth time, Sis whispered to Trish, who was sitting in front of her, "What are you going to wear?" Sis yearned for her best friend's company. But Trish just ignored her.

Early on rehearsal day, the six Lake School contestants waited nervously inside the state capital's Performing Arts Center. When they heard the announcement on the loudspeaker: "Lake School, Jasper," Sis whispered, "Break a leg, Trish." But Trish ignored Sis once again.

Sis was tired of trying. Now, when the girls needed each other most, their friendship fizzled. The two stood behind the piano together, but they were miles apart. In the silence, Dick began, "A friend . . . ."

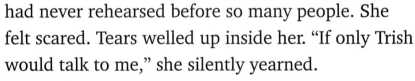

Each finalist had just three minutes. Sis had never rehearsed before so many people. She felt scared. Tears welled up inside her. "If only Trish would talk to me," she silently yearned.

After the rehearsal, the oratory contest's director, John Heart, gathered the students in the auditorium. "We want to congratulate all the finalists. Regardless of who wins tomorrow, you are all winners. Of the thousands who tried out across our state, you're the best!" He suggested one final practice that night in front of a mirror.

The Lake School students from Jasper looked around. They realized just how many other students were vying for the top prize, a five thousand dollar scholarship.

Dick had invited them to watch a movie in the room the boys shared. But when they got back to the hotel, Sis said, "I've seen that movie at least ten times." In the girls' room, Maria Rozas was practicing. Maria, a beautiful sixth grade girl, was another finalist from Lake School. Terribly shy, Maria was more nervous than anyone else.

"Hello, Sis. Hello, Trish," Maria offered. Sis responded, but Trish wasn't speaking to Maria either. Inside this crowded room, Trish felt alone.

The next morning, Sis tried to compose herself. But it was hard to become Auntie Mame and be funny when she was feeling miserable. "I guess this is what actors mean when they say 'the show must go on'," Sis sighed.

As the group split up for the cab ride to the Performing Arts Center, Trish avoided getting into the same taxi with Sis. So Sis rode with Maria and

Mr. Rosenburg while Dick and Trish followed with Miss Pitt and the others.

Sis had been repeating her lines to herself, worrying about how she could make people laugh when she herself was so near tears. Suddenly, a loud screech, honking horns, and a crash of metal rang in Sis's ears. That was the last thing Sis heard. A huge truck had sideswiped them.

Traffic stopped. Cars pulled over to one side, heeding the blaring sirens of an ambulance. Trish tried to get out of the cab, but Miss Pitt made her wait until the EMTs had finished their job.

When she saw the two EMTs lifting the stretcher into the back door of the ambulance, Trish feared the worst. The person on the stretcher was far too small to be Mr. Rosenburg. Or even Maria. It could only be Sis.

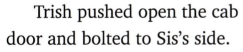

Trish pushed open the cab door and bolted to Sis's side. Inside the back of the ambulance, she bent over Sis. "Sis!" Trish sobbed, "Please speak to me! Sis! My best friend! Please talk to me!"

Steve Rosenburg had to make some quick decisions. "Miss Pitt, you get into the ambulance with Sis and call her parents from the hospital. I'll

call you as soon as I get the others to the Performing Arts Center."

"I'm staying with Sis," Trish said. They tried to encourage her to go with Mr. Rosenburg.

"Trish, you've worked so hard for this!" said Miss Pitt. "I'm sure Sis will be just fine. You have a good chance of winning! Even Pat didn't win in her third grade year."

But Trish was firm in her decision. "I don't care whether Pat won or lost. It's only a contest, and there's always next year." Trish refused to leave her friend's side.

Sis lay there silently, not moving. Trish remembered how she had felt earlier that morning.

As the ambulance raced toward the hospital, Trish spoke to Sis, even though she realized that Sis couldn't hear her. "When I looked into the mirror this morning, I was ashamed of what I saw. You are my best friend, Sis. You will always be my best friend. I was only thinking of myself and of

winning the contest. I was jealous because you were so funny when you did your Auntie Mame speech. I didn't really think I had a chance. You were so good. Oh, please, Sis! Please wake up!"

By the time Mr. and Mrs. Turner arrived at the hospital to see their daughter Sis, her leg had been set in a cast, and the other Lake School students had returned with Mr. Rosenburg to give Sis and Trish the news of the state oratory contest.

Trish was sitting beside Sis on the hospital bed, each with a big bowl of ice cream which the nurse had provided them. Maria and Mr. Rosenburg were recalling Dick's wonderful Julius Caesar presentation. Beaming, Dick wore his red ribbon.

Everyone insisted that Dick had deserved first prize, but it had gone to a student from Huntingburg.

"Please, Dick," urged Sis's dad, Mr. Turner. "Mrs. Turner and I would love to hear your Julius Caesar reading." The request didn't take much urging.

"A friend should bear his friend's infirmities . . ." began Dick.

Sis and Trish looked at each other and smiled secretly.

Vocabulary Expansion

Describe and define these words and phrases:

oratory contest	on her heels	anticipate
follow in her footsteps	tore out	weasel out
early bird catches the worm	badmouth	red ribbon
compose yourself	hypersensitive	worked up
the show must go on	sideswipe	choked up

Language Expansion Activities

1. Ask a librarian to help you locate these volumes: (a) *Great Books*; (b) William Shakespeare's plays, *Julius Caesar* and *Romeo and Juliet* (see if you can find the quotation Dick recited in the story and Juliet's balcony speech); and (c) Patrick Dennis's book, *Auntie Mame*. Memorize a selection from any of these volumes and recite it for your group.

2. Plan an oratory contest for your class. Have the students select poems or selections from stories or plays that they would like to memorize and recite. Ask three of the teachers in your school to be the judges.

Language Expansion Questions

1. Explain the meaning of the story's title *Rehearsal for Friendship*.

2. What did Sis mean when she said, *"I just hope Trish doesn't choke if she gets a chance at the state contest."*? Why did Trish become so angry with Sis? Can misunderstandings ruin friendships?

3. What does "state contest" mean? Where were the students going? Why?

4. Trish was upset because everyone always compared her to her older sister. Does anyone ever compare you to anyone else? How does it make you feel?

5. The students raced back from lunch to see the names of the finalists posted on the classroom door. How did the winners feel? The losers? Have you ever had to wait for the results of a contest? How did you feel?

6. Explain the meaning of this passage: *"The two stood behind the piano together, but they were miles apart."*

7. Imagine what might have happened if Sis hadn't been hurt. Write a different ending for the story. Share your ending with the others in your group.

8. What do you think Trish and Sis learned from their experience? Explain how they came to change the way they felt about each other and about the state oratory contest.

9. Many stories have heroes and villains. Discuss who you think was the hero in this story. Was there a villain? Explain your opinions.

10. Mr. Rosenburg and Miss Pitt stayed after school and helped the six students perfect their readings. Name a teacher who has gone out of the way to help you. List that teacher's good characteristics. What makes this kind of teacher so great?

Unit 40

A NARROW ESCAPE

UNIT 40

Phonology/Orthography Concepts

- Phonology/orthography for sound pattern /*air*/:
  - Phonograms are letter groups that usually represent the same sounds (phonemes).
  - However, **six different** letter groups can represent the sound pattern /*air*/: **air**, **ear**, **are**, **er**, **err**, **arr**.

Vocabulary

aircraft	chair	hair	sparrow	*imagine*
airline	chairman	herring	square	*engine*
airmail	cherry	merit	stair	*island*
airport	compare	merry	stare	
arrow	dairy	narrow	swear	
bare	dare	pair	tear	
barrel	Derrick	parent	terrible	
bear	errand	parrot	there	
berry	error	pear	vary	
care	fair	prepare	very	
careful	fairway	scare	wear	
carrot	farewell	sheriff	where	
carry	flair	spare		

A NARROW ESCAPE

Story Summary:

Nick Hopkins and his scout troop are spending the day at the renovated airport, and visiting the new air traffic control tower. His little brother, Bud, wants to go too. Before the day ends, he manages to completely disrupt airport services.

"Mom," Bud Hopkins called loudly as he soared down the stairs, "can I ride out to the airport on my bike? I'll be careful. I'll look both ways."

"Certainly not," said his mom as Bud slid into the kitchen wearing his new bearclaw slippers.

"The airport is miles away, and besides, you promised your father that you would rake up some leaves this morning." Mrs. Hopkins poured him some cereal and told Bud to sit down for breakfast.

"Aw, Mom!" Bud whined, "can't I just go out there for a minute? I really want to see the new air traffic control tower and jet runways. Anyway, Nick and the scouts get to go." Nick was Bud's older brother. Nick was 13 now, and he seemed to be permitted to do everything that eight-year old Bud could not.

"Well," Mrs. Hopkins suggested as she cut up a pear for Bud, "I imagine you could convince your cub scout troop to go out there on a field trip. I wouldn't mind if you went with a supervised group."

Bud stared at his cereal bowl. "Why do my parents treat me like a baby?" he thought to himself.

"Good morning, Mom! Hey there, short stuff!" Nick exclaimed, pulling another chair up to the kitchen table. "What's for breakfast? I'm starved and I've only got three minutes to eat."

"Good morning, Nick," replied Mrs. Hopkins. "Your hair looks nice, but shouldn't you be wearing your uniform? I thought there was something about you scouts having to wear uniforms on troop expeditions."

"Chill out, Mom," Nick retorted teasingly. "Mr. Bell said we didn't have to wear our uniforms. Besides, it's Saturday."

"Do you think Mr. Bell would let me go along?" suggested Bud, wiping milk off his chin. "I could carry the backpacks or something."

"No way, José," retorted Nick. "Nobody's allowed to take any brothers or sisters." Nick downed his cereal and stuffed a pear and some cherry candy into his scout pack.

"Hasta luego," bellowed Nick, barreling out the back door. Nick was learning Spanish from his

friend, Nando. When Nando had first arrived, he could speak English fairly well, but could barely read or write it. Nick had helped him. Now Nick and Nando were a pair, and someone else was feeling left out.

Since kindergarten, Al Long had been Nick's best friend. It was Al who had spent his spare time helping Nick prepare for tests. When nobody else had seemed to care, Al had been there for Nick.

As he flew along the path that paralleled Airline Highway, Bud Hopkins' hair stood on end. He kept trying to convince himself that what he was doing was only fair. After all, the opening ceremony for the new international jet air service to Latin America and the Caribbean would only be this morning. He had plenty of time to get home and rake leaves. Nobody would even know he was gone.

"Hey, kid, where do you think you're going! You gave me a scare!" A car had pulled up beside him, and a man was shouting at Bud. "Bikes aren't permitted on the airport access road!" The man gunned his accelerator and took off.

Bud guided his bike over the low railing and under a barbed wire fence, back into an area just behind a giant dairy sign. Staring at the huge tear in his new jeans, he thought, "I guess I'll leave my bike here; nobody will see it."

Bud trudged toward the runways, and spotted a giant silver plane in line for takeoff. "I'll just slip under this fence," he thought.

The scouts always met in front of Lake School, where Ken Bell picked them up in his van to go on field trips. When Nick and Nando got there on their bikes, Al had already arrived. He was talking to Sam Webster and Sid North. Mat Miller was pedaling up Tenth Street Hill.

"Yo! Al! Sam! Sid!" Nick greeted his old friends.

Nando had become a member of the troop during the summer, but the others still considered him a newcomer. At first, Nick imagined that Al wasn't his usual friendly self, but he decided it was just that—his imagination. There was a flair about Nick. Everyone liked

him. But sometimes, Nick wasn't aware of the very thing in front of his face.

Ken Bell, the scout leader, had arranged for his scout troop to visit the airport terminal and jetway, and to go up into the new air traffic control tower. One of Ken's friends, an airline pilot, was escorting them. Over the years, this troop had had many adventures. Ken Bell was a fine leader who prepared the boys for life.

When they were cub scouts, he'd taught them to tie square knots; in later years, he'd helped them prepare to earn their merit badges; in sixth grade, he'd taken them on a tall sailing ship; and each summer they'd gone camping. Ken Bell was like another parent to his scouts, and they respected him.

Ken's pilot friend had gotten them a special parking pass. When the van pulled into the VIP lot, the boys were excited. The high-pitched whir of jet engines created images of faraway places, and these scouts were true explorers. They had learned how to be daring and careful at the same time. More than anything, they wanted to

see the world and everything in it.

Sheriff's deputies strolled throughout the terminal to ensure security. Derrick Waring, the pilot, escorted them through a special entrance into the pilot's lounge to give them a briefing. These boys had been learning all about air traffic control, and were excited to see it in action.

"Even a minor error in air traffic control can mean life or death," Derrick explained. "The new flights out of here and into Latin America, the Caribbean, and the Canary Islands mean increased traffic. Under no circumstances may you interrupt the people in the ATC tower. Understood? The chairman of the Aviation Board is here today, and has agreed to speak to us after lunch. Let's go."

Inside the ATC tower, the scouts could see for miles. Runways looked like sidewalks; jets looked like model planes. Computerized radar screens provided the air traffic controllers with critical information, especially in times of low visibility.

Nick wished he could ask Al how it all worked. Al was a computer whiz, and he had always been able to explain things in ways that other people could understand. Nick admired Al more than anyone else he knew.

Meanwhile, Bud Hopkins was feeling a little scared. He'd crawled under a fence that gave him a little shock, and now he was on the pavement. He couldn't find a way to get off, so he decided to walk along the fence until he got near the terminal building. Then he'd have to find a way to get inside the building, so that he could get back out, find his bike, and get home in time to rake up all those leaves. By now, Bud had forgotten the imagined thrill of the day.

A huge aircraft was taxiing along the runway, and the thundering noise forced Bud to crouch down and cover his ears with his arms. When it left the ground, Bud scurried along beside the fence as fast as he could, longing to find a way into the terminal. But he could see that all of the ramp employees and baggage handlers wore official uniforms and headgear. How could he possibly get inside the security-proof terminal without being discovered? Discovery was out. "If my parents ever find out," Bud mumbled to himself, "I'll be punished for life." This was a problem with no solution.

 On their way down in the huge glass elevator of the new ATC tower, Al Long shouted, "Nick! Look over there! On the pavement! It's Bud!" The boys stared in shock, along with Ken and Derrick.

"Let's get these kids back inside the terminal fast, Ken. I've got to get to a security phone!" Derrick Waring's voice sounded like an alarm.

Just when he thought there was no hope of ever getting back home, Bud spotted a baggage mover with wide leather straps that looked something like his grandfather Hopkins' treadmill, only much bigger. Bags were being routed from a baggage cart outside an aircraft that had just landed, straight into the terminal building. Bud thought of the terrible punishment he could avoid, if only he could get himself onto one of those baggage movers and into the terminal. Once inside that building, he would be safe.

The boys decided to break up into pairs and search the terminal building for the next hour, in the hope that they would find Bud. "Let's meet under the clock at the main entrance at 12:30," instructed Ken Bell. "Don't leave any section of this building unsearched. Bud could enter anywhere."

"And I've alerted the airport emergency patrol," added Derrick. "They know there's a little kid out there on the runways—somewhere."

Nick was glad that Ken had paired him with Al Long. Everybody had always thought of Al as a sort of detective. "Come on, Nick," Al said. We'll find him. I know just where to look."

"What do you mean, Al? I mean, the kid could be anyplace. Bud and his friends have gotten into some jams together before. But nothing like this. I mean, nobody can ever predict what they're going to get into. And they're not bad kids. They just don't think." Nick was not convinced that Al could lead them to Bud, but he was willing to follow Al, knowing his track record.

"Over there, Nick. Take the escalator down to the lowest level," directed Al. "Move fast." The two of them moved to the far left of the escalator and trotted briskly down the moving stairway. Both Nick and Al were in good shape. They were cross-country runners on their

school's track team. The renovated terminal was unfamiliar to Al, but he followed the signs and eventually said, "OK, Nick. This is it. I predict that Bud will arrive within minutes."

"Sure, Al. Bud's going to find us in this huge airport?" Nick thought Al was being a little overdramatic in his detective role.

By now, two messages had been announced. All air traffic had stopped. No planes could take off, and planes in the air had been instructed from the ATC tower to circle overhead until the boy was found. After all, a huge aircraft would not be able to avoid a child. What nobody could figure out was how Bud had gotten onto the runways in the first place, with intense security all over the terminal.

Bud was scared. He'd managed to slip onto the mammoth baggage mover, between some canvas bags marked *U.S. Post Office: Airmail* and a big steamer trunk. This thing was moving lots faster than it had first appeared to. Ahead, light filtered through giant black rubber strips hanging from a small square opening in the wall.

He had no idea what was ahead; he just scrunched down and waited.

"I don't believe it!" Nick Hopkins exclaimed. "This is too much, Al. Even for you." From where the two stood, they had seen the conveyor belt begin to move, returning baggage to passengers. There, on the conveyor belt, sat Bud. The travelers began cheering. Al had already run up to retrieve Bud, who was like a little brother to him.

Bud Hopkins wasn't certain whether he should feel terrified or elated. He was sure getting lots of attention. People were taking his picture, and lots of grownups were laughing. They didn't seem too mad. Maybe his mom and dad wouldn't be mad, either. His new jeans were in tatters by now, and he realized that he had no idea how to find his bike.

By the time the rest of the troop heard the announcement that Bud had been found and that air traffic had resumed, Nick and Al had delivered Bud to the troop's meeting place under the clock. Nick just shook his head. "Bud, Bud, Bud. I'll never understand how you pulled this one off!"

Vocabulary Expansion

Describe and define these words and phrases:

hasta luego	hair stood on end	low visibility
pull one off	gunned the accelerator	air traffic control
chill out	the very thing in front of his face	reconnoiter
short stuff	under no circumstances	ATC tower
overdramatic	terminal building	baggage claim
taxiing	track record	area
VIP parking lot	critical information	radar

Language Expansion Activities

1. Have each individual in your group call a different airline or find one on the Internet. Ask them to send you information about the routes they travel. (Airlines have free 1-800 telephone numbers.) Then, trace the airlines' routes on a map. Give a group oral report explaining which airlines fly which routes. Include information about which cities are hubs for the different airlines. Explain why it is necessary for airlines to have hub cities. Investigate which airlines have flights into Latin America, the Canary Islands, and the Caribbean Islands. Locate those places on a map or globe.

2. Investigate the work of air traffic controllers. Compare their jobs with other jobs that people do. Write a report on the way that they use radar to help direct traffic. Explain why air traffic controllers' jobs are called high-stress jobs. Discuss the ways that a stressful job could influence someone's life. Invite an air traffic controller to visit your school's career day.

Language Expansion Questions

1. What kinds of activities did Nick's scout troop do? If you were a scout, what special activities would you like to plan?

2. How did Bud feel when his big brother took off for an exciting day? Do you think Nick was unfair in not letting Bud go? Have you ever had to refuse a younger brother or sister? Have you ever been refused by an older brother or sister? Explain how you felt.

3. Explain how Bud accidentally got onto the runway. Was Bud bad? Explain how good people can sometimes get into bad trouble. What are the best ways of avoiding situations like Bud's?

4. Create other possible endings for this story, in which there might have been tragedy. Bud was worried about how his parents might respond when they heard what had happened. What is the difference between their probable punishment of Bud and a true tragedy?

5. An airline pilot's job is important. What type of person would make a good pilot? What characteristics would he or she need?

6. If you were Al, how would you have felt at the beginning of the story? How would you have felt at the end? Why? What will happen with Nick and Al? Can you have more than one best friend?

7. The others had known each other since kindergarten, but Nando had just moved there. Why is it hard for someone who moves into a new city or town to make friends? Can new people feel accepted?

8. Nick didn't know how Al figured out Bud's arrival spot. How did Al draw his conclusion? Why do the others think of Al as a detective?

9. Why did the scouts plan to meet under the clock at a particular time? Have you ever been with a group that planned a reconnoiter?

10. Imagine that you are the pilot, Derrick Waring. Tell this story from his point of view.

Unit 41

SABOTAGE AT THE INTERNATIONALS

UNIT 41

Phonology/Orthography Concepts

- Orthography/phonology for schwa /∂/:
  - The schwa phoneme /∂/ may be represented by any of these vowel letters (graphemes): **a**, **e**, **i**, **o**, or **u**.
  - The schwa is found most often:
    1) When **a** begins or ends a word of more than one syllable
    2) In the second syllable of a two-syllable word
    3) In an unaccented syllable of a multi-syllable word

Vocabulary

abandon	arrange	barrel	kitchen	*change*
ability	arrive	beacon	legend	*child*
accommodate	assist	bottom	lion	*clothes*
account	atomic	Carbon	marshall	*most*
across	attack	celebrate	multiply	*pint*
address	attend	cobra	opera	*post*
affect	attendant	comma	orphan	*pull*
afford	attention	consider	panda	*push*
agree	attract	consult	parrot	
alone	authority	contain	penetrate	
amaze	avoid	convince	permanent	
anthem	awake	denim	pilot	
appear	away	dynamite	pollution	
applaud	bacon	elephant	quota	tuna
appoint	balance	engine	ransom	vacant
approach	balcony	extra	rascal	wagon
apron	ballot	focus	salad	weapon
arena	banana	gallop	seven	woman
around	barnacle	infant	soda	zebra

SABOTAGE AT THE INTERNATIONALS

Story Summary:

Molly Manchester has just won the USA Junior Girls' Equestrian Trotting Finals, and is on her way to England to compete in the World Cup. Everything is going smoothly until sabotage ruins Molly's chances.

"But, Mom," Molly insisted, "I can't possibly win without Lady. She's just got to go!"

"I didn't say that Lady couldn't go," Mrs. Manchester replied. "You're not listening to me."

Molly Manchester had just won the USA Junior Girls' Equestrian Trotting Finals. She had begun competing in equestrian events more than seven years ago. It was a way for Molly to get to know people in new communities since her father, a U.S. Army officer, traveled and their family had to move so often. Molly had lived all over the world. She had learned to ride at the age of four in Arabia. Molly's horse, Lady, was an Arabian beauty. Now Molly was planning a trip to London, England, where she would compete in the World Cup.

"We're very proud of you, Honey," Mrs. Manchester went on, "and your father and I will support you all the way. But you have to be reasonable about Lady. Lady will have to go by ship, not plane. She must leave a week before we do."

"Oh," Molly said shyly, "sorry, Mom. I guess I was just so excited that I couldn't even concentrate."

"Dad will meet us at Gatwick Airport, London," her mother said. "Lady will be shipped directly to the ASCOT stables. We have reservations at the hotel three weeks from Monday."

"I just wish Dad could be here to celebrate with us," Molly mused. "He *was* the one who taught me to ride. I miss him so much, Mom."

"Dad is always with us," Mrs. Manchester maintained, "even when he's posted elsewhere for awhile. So where shall we go to celebrate?"

"Could we go to the ballet? *Romeo and Juliet* is playing, and it's my favorite!" Molly urged.

"Sure, Honey," Mrs. Manchester replied. "And I'll spring for dinner, too. How about Chinese food? I've heard that the new restaurant in town is excellent."

"Sounds great, Mom," Molly said. "Could Tam and Pat come along? After all, they convinced me to enter the competition in the first place."

"Okay, but they'll have to be ready by seven!"

"Dynamite! Don't worry, Mom," Molly answered gaily. "I'm going upstairs to call them right now.

Hope I can find something incredible to wear. I'll need just the right thing for *Romeo and Juliet*!"

On the way home from the ballet, the girls stared dreamily out the car window.

"Romeo, Romeo, wherefore art thou? And why can't you ever appear in Jasper?" Pat mused.

"Likely," Tam sighed. "Anyway, we'll sure miss you, Molly. You'll have to write us. Tell us all about the other girls in the show."

"Don't worry," Molly answered Tam. "You two will be the first to know."

Three weeks passed slowly for Molly, but the day finally arrived to leave for England. Mrs. Manchester was preparing their luggage tags. "Did your bags suddenly multiply, Molly?" her mom asked. "Last time I checked, you only had two."

"But I really *need* four," Molly pleaded. "I just couldn't get all my clothes into two bags. I have my jodhpurs for the contest. I need good clothes for the victory dinner. Plus accessories for everything!"

"Well, it's a good thing *I* only have two," Mrs. Manchester chided. "We'll be OK."

Heading down Airline Highway, Molly noticed that the airport door was decorated with balloons and a banner: "*Molly Manchester: Equestrian Champion of the World!*" It seemed that the whole ninth grade class had turned out to wish Molly good luck. Tam and Pat presented Molly with a bouquet of flowers.

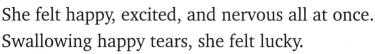

As the plane headed down the runway, Molly could still spot most of her friends waving inside the terminal. She felt happy, excited, and nervous all at once. Swallowing happy tears, she felt lucky.

Molly hurried down the exit ramp at Gatwick Airport. She only had eyes for her father. Colonel Manchester ran up the ramp. A family hug found the three Manchesters celebrating their reunion. "Did you get Lady yet, Dad?" questioned Molly.

"Lady has been stalled for three days now," replied her father. "I thought you would want to see her now," he added, "so I've arranged for a taxi."

"Thanks, Dad," Molly smiled, relieved. "It means a lot to me."

As they entered ASCOT's competitors' lounge, Molly and her family were introduced to other World Cup participants. Suddenly, Molly came face to face with her chief competition, Vanessa Carbon of Australia. Vanessa was recognized in girls' equestrian competition as best in her class. "It's nice to meet you," Molly declared, quietly sizing her up.

"How delightful!" Vanessa was a tall, regal-looking girl with waist-length, silky blond hair.

The two girls chatted at length about the contest. Molly liked Vanessa, but soon realized she hadn't checked Lady yet. She quickly excused herself and rushed to the stables. When Molly got there, she whispered to Lady, "We're going to win this contest, old girl. I just feel it in my bones!" Molly had never felt this confident before. Maybe it was because she was so happy to be back with Lady.

Just then, Molly noticed a strange woman crouched in the corner of Lady's stall, fingering through the hay. "May I help you with something?" Molly asked.

"Oh! You must be Molly Manchester. I can't believe that *you* are the one my daughter Vanessa is so concerned about beating!" blurted the woman.

"I am Molly Manchester," Molly announced. "And you must be Mrs. Carbon."

"Yes, dear," she went on, "I'm Elvira Carbon. I was anxious to meet both you and your horse. I understand the horse is a prize Arabian. Of course, she couldn't be *near* the caliber horse my Vanessa will be riding."

"Her name is Lady," Molly said with pride. "And she is a *beautiful* horse." Molly went on, "Why are you in Lady's stable?" Molly wanted to know how this rude woman had gotten into Lady's stall.

"I just stopped to admire your horse and I seem to have lost an earring." Mrs. Carbon continued, "You do understand, my dear, that Vanessa is way out of your league. She's won the World Cup twice before! I really *must* go now. *Ever* so much luck tomorrow. Let me know if you find that earring."

"I'll do that," Molly stated matter-of-factly.

As Mrs. Carbon turned to go, she brushed past a groom coming into the stable. Molly thought she

saw Mrs. Carbon tuck a small bottle into her jacket pocket. "Poor Vanessa! What an awful mother!" thought Molly.

Just then, Molly's parents arrived. "How's the world's best trotter?" smiled her father.

"Well," Molly replied, "according to Mrs. Carbon, Lady isn't worth entering at all!"

"What are you talking about?" her father asked.

"Mrs. Carbon was here," Molly said. "She told me not to bother entering tomorrow. She said that Vanessa and her horse were 'out of my class'."

"Never mind her, darling," encouraged the Colonel. "You'll convince them all tomorrow!"

Colonel Manchester treated his family to a royal feast. They dined on the balcony of an elegant restaurant overlooking Picadilly Circus in London's West End. Horses continued to be the main topic of conversation.

Molly recognized Vanessa at another table and waved to her. "Oh, no," she gasped, "that awful Mrs. Carbon is coming over here."

"Colonel Manchester, I presume," Mrs. Carbon said holding out a limp hand, "I'm Elvira Carbon."

"Indeed." Colonel Manchester replied. "May I introduce my lovely wife, Faith."

"Charmed, I'm sure," cooed Mrs. Carbon. She teased Molly, "Preparing for your first defeat, dear?"

Molly was about to stand up when her dad gently held her down. "We'll see!" he said. "I think our Molly is going to surprise you, Mrs. Carbon."

"I can tell you've never seen my Vanessa," retorted Mrs. Carbon as she turned toward her table.

At 9:00 the next morning, Molly and her family were in the arena waiting for Lady. They were all taken aback when the groom rushed up. "Lady is lying down and not responding," he cried.

"Daddy, what's happened to Lady?" Molly cried out as she rushed into the stables. "Why is she on the ground? She's not breathing right. Oh, Daddy, why? Why? What could have happened?"

"We'll have to wait and consult the vet," Colonel Manchester said as he tried to soothe her. But Molly was inconsolable. She could hear the blast of trumpets playing the anthem that signaled the start of the events. Lying down next to her horse, Molly sobbed.

Upon examination, the vet announced that she felt Lady may have been drugged. "I'm not convinced," Dr. Kaplan explained, "but all the symptoms indicate foul play. I will have to send blood samples to the lab for confirmation. I feel certain that Lady will come around, but she will not be entering any competitions for quite a while."

The Colonel was stunned. "Why would anyone want to drug Lady?" he asked out loud. Colonel Manchester headed toward the phones. "Inspector Stacey at Scotland Yard owes me a favor," he thought as he phoned the number.

Later that morning, Colonel Manchester explained the situation to Inspector Charles Stacey and his partner, Harold Beacon.

Inspector Stacey and his partner questioned Molly and the groom at length about what had happened. Molly couldn't remember much until the groom reminded her of Mrs. Carbon's visit to the stables the evening before. "You remember, now, don't you love?" queried the groom. "That woman was in Lady's stable when you arrived, wasn't she?"

"That's right," Molly remembered, "and just before she left, I saw her put something like a small bottle back into her coat pocket. Oh! Daddy! Do you think Mrs. Carbon had anything to do with it?"

"We'll let the detectives do their work, Molly. Our job is to stay here and be with Lady." Colonel Manchester tried to console his daughter.

"You've been very helpful, Molly," assured Inspector Stacey. "But your father's right. We'll investigate and then get back to you."

In the background, Molly could hear the voice on the loudspeaker announcing the posting event. Just then, the vet reappeared in the stables. "I was right about Lady," she confirmed. "She was drugged. I have the antidote with me, though, so Lady should be up and about in a few hours."

Later, Molly could hear the trumpets signaling the end of the international events. The loudspeaker announced that Vanessa had won. At that moment, Lady got up on all fours. "Oh, Lady," Molly cried out joyfully, "you're going to be OK!"

Later that afternoon, Inspector Stacey arrived at the Strand. He began, "I want you to be the first to know that we have arrested Elvira Carbon for drugging your horse. The chambermaid found a vial in her room. The drug is identical to the one that the vet said had been given to your horse, Lady. Mrs. Carbon confessed just minutes ago."

"Mr. Carbon and Vanessa were both shocked to learn about Mrs. Carbon's actions," the inspector continued. "We'll be taking her to Scotland Yard for further questioning."

As Inspector Stacey was leaving, Vanessa appeared at the Manchesters' door. "Molly," she was in tears, "I'm so sorry! I just can't believe my mother could do such a thing. Here's the trophy. You're the one who deserves it."

Molly wanted to reach for the sterling silver World Cup trophy. She had come 3,000 miles to try to win it. But she could not accept it. Through her tears, Molly sobbed, "It's not your fault, Vanessa. I'm just sorry we couldn't have competed. You'd probably have won. I just wanted a chance." The two girls hugged and pledged one day to compete.

Vanessa was as heartbroken as Molly.

Later that evening, when Vanessa had gone, Molly couldn't help longing for her good friends and home. Sharing this story with Tam, Pat, and Kim would be almost as good as winning the World Cup. Almost. But not quite.

Vocabulary Expansion

Describe and define these words and phrases:

equestrian	world traveler	competition
posted	pavilion	arena
antagonist	sizing one up	feel it in my bones
subvert	near the caliber	out of one's league
inconsolable	foul play	narcotic

Language Expansion Activities

1. Write Mrs. Carbon's story. Be sure to include her reasons for wanting Vanessa to win so badly that she would stoop to sabotage. Explain how she gets along with her daughter and her husband. What kind of a woman is she?

2. Pretend that you are going to London for a competition. What kind of competition would you choose? What kinds of things would you need to take with you? Make a list. Compare it with the lists of others in your group.

Language Expansion Questions

1. What kind of competition was Molly entering? Why?

2. Molly and her mother were going to London by plane. How did Lady get there? How did Molly's father get there?

3. Where did Molly and her mother and friends go to celebrate? Would you have chosen that kind of celebration? Where would you go for a big celebration? Why?

4. How many important events in this story can you remember? Have your teacher time you and try to write down as many as you can in two minutes. Compare your list with the lists of others in your group.

5. Molly didn't like Mrs. Carbon much. What are some of the things Mrs. Carbon did to Molly to make her feel that way? Do you know anyone who makes you feel that way? Explain.

6. Imagine what could have happened if Mrs. Carbon hadn't drugged Lady. Write a new ending for the story.

7. What is a groom? Why is he or she an important person at a stable? What are some of his or her duties? Who are some of the other important people at an arena?

8. Horses are entered in competitions. What other kinds of animals are entered in competitions? Where are they taken to compete? Why are animal owners so protective?

9. Can you explain why Mrs. Carbon committed a crime? Do you think people can do bad things because they love somebody?

10. Describe the qualities you would look for in the perfect mother.

Unit 42
ACCUSATION

UNIT 42

Phonology/Orthography Concepts

- Phonograms are letter groups that usually represent the same sounds (phonemes).
  - The phonograms **tion**, **sion**, **cian**, **xion**, and **tien** represent the sound pattern /*shun*/.
  - The phonograms **xious** and **cious** represent the sound pattern /*shus*/.
  - The phonogram **sion** represents the sound pattern /*zhun*/ after a vowel or an **r**.

Vocabulary

anxious	election	physician	*iron*
application	excursion	politician	*onion*
caution	explosion	pollution	
combination	expression	precious	
complexion	gracious	procession	
condition	immersion	profession	
confession	impression	quotient	
confusion	intervention	secession	
conversion	invention	spacious	
decision	magician	subtraction	
delicious	multiplication	succession	
digestion	musician	tension	
diversion	omission	transmission	
division	patient	transportation	
efficient	permission	version	

ACCUSATION

Story Summary:

Nando is accused, and several students consider him guilty without searching for the truth. They discover what it means to be accused and found guilty without due process.

There was division at Tenth Street School. Yesterday, an explosion had destroyed Nick Hopkins' locker, just outside Mr. Ade's office. Today, tension filled the air. No student had made a confession, but some had the impression that Fernando Rozas had committed the crime. Others stood behind Nando. They knew him to be a fine person of strong ethics.

Sam Webster was amazed. People who were friends yesterday were bitter enemies today. He and Sid North spoke to Mr. Cooper, the custodian, at lunchtime. "Only a magician coulda' gotten in those doors," Coop had told them. "Only person I let in here after school was that foreign kid, hangs around with Nick Hopkins. You ask me, he's the one that done it. Nobody else coulda' got in here. Woulda' had ta' known the school's night lock combination. Nobody knows that 'cept me 'n' the principal. His office has a night lock, too. Even I can't get in his office. Not with his night lock on. It was that kid, all right."

Some thought the explosion was the work of a professional criminal. But why would anyone blow up a student's locker? The police began their investigation, calling a constant procession of students and teachers into the principal's office. Whose version of the truth would they accept? Now, Sam and Sid awaited their turns. They didn't know anything. They'd gone over to Pat's after school to work on their project for the science fair.

"I don't like this, Sam. Just because Nando came back here to get his English book doesn't mean he's guilty. Like, what if we got accused every time we came back to school to get something that we'd forgotten?" Sid North planned to be a defense lawyer, and he always tried to see both sides of an issue. The two sat waiting outside Mr. Ade's office.

"I know, Sid. But think of it. Nando was the only one who got back into school after Coop locked up. Nando *must* have done it. I can't believe he'd do it, Sid, but the evidence points to it." Sam liked Nando, and found it hard to believe him guilty. Besides, Nando and Nick were friends. But there was no other way it could have happened, it seemed.

Just then, Nando exited the office, wearing an expression of dejection. He glanced at Sam and Sid, who greeted him with caution. They weren't certain if he'd overheard their conversation. They felt awkward, and just a little guilty for not standing up for their new friend one hundred percent. Sam looked up. Nick and Nando stood near Nick's ruined locker, just outside Mr. Ade's office door.

Nick yanked Nando's arm. "Come on, buddy," he said. "We're out of here." Nick had been elected class president, and could usually influence others. This time, though, he seemed to have lost his power of persuasion. The students were divided. Few supported Nando, even though Nick did.

"Webster! North!" a burly old police officer pushed the office door wide open. "Maybe you two can help us out here. Who wants to come first?"

Sid North felt anxious. He picked up his books and entered the office. He knew that Nando had an uncle on the police force. Sid had made a decision to be completely open. He might know something that could help clear Nando.

Sam waited in the hall. He felt queasy. That delicious spaghetti he'd eaten for lunch today was making itself felt. When he got an upset stomach, his mother always said, "It's just your digestion." Whatever it was, digestion or not, Sam felt awful.

Sid sat on the couch. "Did you see that locker out there?" the officer inquired of Sid. "Got any idea who could have blown it up?" He waited. "Well, son. Don't you have any ideas? None at all?"

"No sir! But, like, we went over to Pat Marks' house after school yesterday to work on our science fair project. Then about 6:00, Mr. Marks drove us both home." Sid's voice trembled.

"Good. That's a start. Now you go back out in the hall and send your friend in here." Sid left gratefully, and sent Sam in to replace him.

"Whose house did you go to after school?" The officer signaled Sam to sit down on the couch.

"Pat Marks. Her dad's on the school board," Sam offered, hoping he wouldn't have to talk again.

"And if I call this Marks guy, he'll testify that you were at his house until he drove you home at 6:00?"

questioned the older officer. Sam began to feel as if he and Sid were the targets of the investigation. "Is there anybody else who could verify that you were there from after school until he drove you home at 6:00?"

"There were six of us there," Sam said. "We're working on an antipollution project for the science fair. Sid and Pat and I were there, and Al Long, Tam Turner, and Kim Chung. Molly Manchester is in our group, too, but she was at a horse contest."

"Are you getting this all down, Anderson?" the officer barked at his partner. He spoke as gruffly to Anderson, the younger officer, as he had to Sam. Sam decided that it was just his means of expression.

Sam gazed around the spacious principal's office. He was hot and his clothes were starting to feel damp. There was precious little air in here. Even though he couldn't see himself, he knew that his complexion was getting more and more pale.

That was the last thing he remembered when he woke up ten minutes later, on the principal's couch. Mr. Wood, his history teacher, held a paper cup and was encouraging him to take a sip of water. He could hear Kim Chung saying, "I called Sam's mom. She'll be here in a minute to pick him up."

"Look! He's coming out of it!" Sam was confused. His buddies, Mat and Sid, stood beside him. Sam's fainting had broken the tension, if only for a few minutes. Mr. Wood offered, "I'll get him a little more water. He can take it with him in the car." A water dispenser sat next to the couch.

When the police officers resumed the investigation, Officer Anderson warned the other students, "Don't make light of this. Whoever did it could do it again—and worse."

Mat Miller was rushing home today because his mom had an appointment with her physician, and he had to watch his baby sister, Joy, a child one-year-old child. The Millers had bought a huge old house down by the dock, near his dad's seafood store. They had been fixing it up, little by little.

Mat loved the new house, but it was a long way to and from school. Just as Mat turned from the bottom of Tenth Street Hill onto Water Street, his back tire blew. "Great!" he thought. "Now I've had it. Leave yourself plenty of time to get home, and your stupid bike tire blows. My parents will kill me."

Mat hesitated to push his bike, because he didn't want to damage his rim. But he only had about a block and a half to go. He would lift the back of the bike and roll it home on the front wheel. It was a little awkward, but it would work.

Mat reached into his basket to take out his backpack and slip it on. That would take some weight off the front wheel and make the bike easier to handle. Lying crushed underneath the backpack, he noticed an orange paper cup. "Where could that have come from?" he wondered. The cup looked familiar, but his mind was on other things, so he slipped on his backpack, leaving the cup in his basket.

It wasn't until much later that evening that he thought of the cup again. When his mom got home from the doctor, Mat took the bike over to the service station at the dock, so he could get a tire patch and fill his tire back up. Riding home, he saw Nick and Nando outside Jen Wells's Pet Shop.

"Hey, Mat!" Nick yelled, "Did you hear? They aren't going to press charges against Nando. There's not enough evidence."

"Don't be so optimistic," Nando stated glumly. "The truth is, if we don't find out who really blew up your locker, I'll be charged. They don't even suspect anybody else."

"I'm sorry, Nando," Mat declared. "Is there anybody you can think of who might have wanted to do it?" Mat sincerely felt sorry for Nando.

Suddenly, Nando's eyes lit up. "Mat! See that orange cup in your basket? Now I remember!" Nando was so excited he started speaking in Spanish.

"Hold up," Nick yelped. "Whoa! Say that again, so we can understand!"

Excitedly, Nando began again, "When Mr. Wood got a cup like that for Sam from the principal's office today, I knew I had seen one just like it before! See! It says, *Jasper Centennial*. It's the same kind of cup

Mr. Cooper had yesterday afternoon when I left school with my English book!"

"So?" Mat and Nick didn't see the connection.

"But that's just it! Don't you see?" Nando explained. "Like, Mr. Cooper *had* to have been in Mr. Ade's office after school yesterday. There's no place else he could have gotten a cup like that!"

"But couldn't he have gotten a cup *before* Mr. Ade put the night lock on his office?" asked Mat.

"No! See! I was at my locker, right outside Mr. Ade's office," Nando went on, "digging around for my English book, while this man was talking to Mr. Ade in his office. He had these orange cups. Brand new. They just got them printed to tell people about the centennial next summer. He even put them in the dispenser. They left together and Mr. Ade put the night lock on his office."

"I still don't get it," Nick contended. "There's a million holes in that theory. Why couldn't Coop have gotten the cup while they were in the office?"

"He wasn't in there," Nando declared. "After Mr. Ade left, I was digging in my locker for my English book. I couldn't find it. Finally, it turned up in the

bottom of Nick's locker—it's right beside mine—under his gym clothes. Just as I pulled my book out, Coop came by. He said to hurry up because he was leaving. When Coop saw me at Nick's locker, he thought it was *my* locker! He planned to blow up my locker, so I'd look guilty! Coop was holding an orange cup. When we left the building together, he dropped it into Mat's bike basket. Remember, Mat! You locked your bike up at school. You were running in the track meet!"

"Coop *had* to have been in that office *after* Mr. Ade put his night lock on!" Nick was excited for Nando.

"Right!" Mat put two and two together. "It was getting dark when we got back from the meet, so I didn't notice the cup. I just dumped my stuff in my basket and rode home." Mat Miller had been carrying around an important clue and didn't even know it! "So Coop really *did* have the combination to Mr. Ade's lock. Even though he said he didn't!"

"It just doesn't make any sense to me, though," Nick commented. "What could Coop stand to gain?"

"I have an idea," Nando replied hesitantly. "I don't know, but . . . . He calls me names, and he's said some stuff to me. Once I heard him say that we didn't need any foreigners in this school. I guess you could say he was pretty mean."

"We need to talk this over with Mr. Ade before we discuss it with anybody else," said Nick.

"We can ride our bikes up to my house. It's just a block away." Mat was glad to help Nando. All three boys were anxious to find out the whole truth.

Mat's dad called Mr. Ade. "This is Chick Miller, George. I hate to bother a tired principal at home, but I think you might want to drive over here and talk to these boys!" he exclaimed.

"There's still a lot I don't understand," Mat's mom said. "How about something to eat while we wait for Mr. Ade to get here? Aren't you kids starved?"

Later, Mr. Ade filled in the missing pieces. "It all makes sense now. That explosion was made with a chemical we use in our science labs. When mixed with ordinary tap water, H_2O, the chemical will explode within fifteen minutes. But I keep all the chemicals locked up in the closet of my office, for safety's sake, so I was certain it couldn't have come from our school. Now we've proved that somebody *did* have the combination to my night lock. I'll have to call the police. They'll want to interview you boys. Chick, can I tell them to come over here? No need to drag these kids down to the police station."

"Let's eat!" Mat Miller would never change.

Vocabulary Expansion

Describe and define these words and phrases:

you can't be totally committed	sometimes	
an expression of dejection	stand up for	accusation
one hundred percent	down in the dumps	interrogation
overheard the conversation	both sides of an issue	testify
the power of persuasion	totally committed	traitors
version of the truth	professional criminal	ethics
be completely open	means of expression	precious little
make light of	resume	queasy
put two and two together	little by little	fixing it up

Language Expansion Activities

1. Plan a mock trial. Select a judge, a prosecutor, and a defense lawyer. Let others play the parts of the witnesses and the accused. Act out a trial that could have resulted from Nando's accusation, if Mat had not accidentally found the clue.

2. In most countries today, people are considered "*innocent until proven guilty.*" They are not necessarily found guilty just because they are accused. In order for a jury to decide that someone is guilty, they must find the person "*guilty beyond a reasonable doubt.*" What do those two phrases mean? Write a story about someone who has been accused of a crime. Use the terms *innocent until proven guilty* and *guilty beyond a reasonable doubt*. Let your story explain how those two ideas can help or hurt someone who has been accused.

Language Expansion Questions

1. Why was Nando accused? How did the students and teachers feel? Discuss Sid's point of view. Sam's. Nick's. Mat's. Explain how the same facts can appear different to different people.

2. Some of this story's characters spoke informally. Does dialectal speech make stories more realistic? Find examples of dialectal speech from books in your school or at home. Share these examples.

3. What happened to Sam in the principal's office? Why did it happen? Recall a time when you have begun to feel queasy.

4. Why was Mr. Ade certain that nobody could get into his office?

5. Nick and Mat had lockers outside Mr. Ade's office. Why was it Nick's locker, and not Nando's, that had been blown up? Recall what was happening when the custodian saw Nando before he left.

6. At first, nobody tried to explain why Nando would have blown up Nick's locker, when Nick was his good friend. Why do you think the police overlooked that important fact?

7. How did Mat accidentally stumble onto the important evidence?

8. How did Mat's flat tire start a chain of events that eventually solved the crime? List *all* the events in the order that they occurred.

9. Coop had called Nando names. Nando hadn't told anybody; he had kept it to himself. Why do you think Coop acted the way he did? Why do you think Nando ignored him?

10. Try to remember a time when you have been absolutely certain about something, and later discovered that you were wrong. Share the event with your group. Explain how you felt when you discovered you were wrong.